Weather Watch

Wind

by Jenny Fretland VanVoorst

Bullfrog
Books

Ideas for Parents and Teachers

Bullfrog Books let children practice reading informational text at the earliest reading levels. Repetition, familiar words, and photo labels support early readers.

Before Reading
- Discuss the cover photo. What does it tell them?
- Look at the picture glossary together. Read and discuss the words.

Read the Book
- "Walk" through the book and look at the photos. Let the child ask questions. Point out the photo labels.
- Read the book to the child, or have him or her read independently.

After Reading
- Prompt the child to think more. Ask: What sorts of things do you like to do outside on windy days?

Bullfrog Books are published by Jump!
5357 Penn Avenue South
Minneapolis, MN 55419
www.jumplibrary.com

Library of Congress Cataloging-in-Publication Data

Names: Fretland VanVoorst, Jenny, 1972– author.
Title: Wind / by Jenny Fretland VanVoorst.
Description: Minneapolis, MN: Jump!, Inc. [2017]
Series: Weather watch | Audience: Ages 5–8.
Audience: K to grade 3. | Includes index.
Identifiers: LCCN 2016011655 (print)
LCCN 2016013476 (ebook)
ISBN 9781620313923 (hardcover: alk. paper)
ISBN 9781624964398 (ebook)
Subjects: LCSH: Winds—Juvenile literature.
Classification: LCC QC931.4 .F74 2017 (print)
LCC QC931.4 (ebook) | DDC 551.51/8—dc23
LC record available at http://lccn.loc.gov/2016011655

Editor: Kirsten Chang
Series Designer: Ellen Huber
Book Designer: Molly Ballanger
Photo Researcher: Molly Ballanger

Photo Credits: All photos by Shutterstock except: Adobe Stock, 8, 14–15, 23br, 23tl; Getty, cover, 3, 4, 5, 16–17, 18–19, 22tl, 22br, 23tr; iStock, 6–7; Thinkstock, 20–21, 22tr.

Printed in the United States of America at Corporate Graphics in North Mankato, Minnesota.

Table of Contents

A Windy Day

Hold onto your hat!

It's a windy day.

What is wind?

Wind is moving air.

You can't see it.

But you can see
what it does.

Look! Grasses bend.

Branches bow.

Leaves blow.

What makes wind?

Warm air rises.

As it rises, it cools.

The cool air falls.

This creates movement.

The movement is wind.

cool air

warm air

Wind is important.
It helps plants.
How?

It spreads seeds around.

seed

Wind moves
weather, too.

A storm forms
on the coast.

But it ends up
in the middle
of the country.

How? Wind.

Wind can cause storms.

But wind can also be fun.

Will flies a kite.

Val goes sailing.

sailboat

What do you do when it's windy?

Types of Wind Storms

hurricane
A powerful storm in which high winds swirl around a calm center.

sandstorm
A storm of wind that drives clouds of sand into the air and across the land.

tornado
A funnel-shaped cloud of whirling wind that moves in a narrow path over the land.

blizzard
A winter storm in which heavy snowfall is blown by strong winds.

Picture Glossary

bow
To bend
into a curve.

sailing
Traveling
over water
in a sailboat.

movement
The act
or process
of moving.

storm
A weather
disturbance with
wind and rain, snow,
hail, sleet, or thunder
and lightning.

Index

To Learn More

Learning more is as easy as 1, 2, 3.

1) Go to www.factsurfer.com

2) Enter "wind" into the search box.

3) Click the "Surf" button to see a list of websites.

With factsurfer.com, finding more information is just a click away.